Night Ride

FASTBACK® Horror

Night Ride

RICHARD LAYMON

GLOBE FEARON
Pearson Learning Group

FASTBACK® HORROR BOOKS

The Caller	The MD's Mistake
The Disappearing Man	Night Games
The Hearse	**Night Ride**
Live Bait	No Power on Earth
The Lonely One	The Rare Shell
The Masterpiece	Tomb of Horror

Cover Eyewire/Getty Images, Inc. All photography © Pearson Education, Inc. (PEI) unless specifically noted.

Copyright © 2004 by Pearson Education, Inc., publishing as Globe Fearon®, an imprint of Pearson Learning Group, 299 Jefferson Road, Parsippany, NJ 07054. All rights reserved. No part of this book may be reproduced or transmitted in any form or by any means, electronic or mechanical, including photocopying, recording, or by any information storage and retrieval system, without permission in writing from the publisher. For information regarding permission(s), write to Rights and Permissions Department.

Globe Fearon® and Fastback® are registered trademarks of Globe Fearon, Inc.

ISBN 0-13-024525-9
Printed in the United States of America
1 2 3 4 5 6 7 8 9 10   07 06 05 04 03

1-800-321-3106
www.pearsonlearning.com

It was the first Friday night of the month. Phil Archer sat down on the bench. The young woman at its other end glanced at him and then leaned forward and peered down the busy avenue. Phil looked, too. The bus was not yet in sight.

Phil turned his eyes to the girl. She leaned back and stared straight ahead. Her blond hair looked silver in the light of the street lamp. It blew gently in the breeze, and so did the collar of her blouse.

Phil watched with pleasure as the headlights of passing cars briefly lit her face. He thought that he had never seen anyone more beautiful.

She was frowning slightly. The bus, as usual, was late. Maybe that was the reason for her worried look. Or maybe she was nervous about Phil staring at her. Even with the frown, though, she was beautiful. She glanced at her wristwatch.

"It's never on time," Phil said.

Her fine eyebrows lifted in surprise. She smiled in a way that made Phil's throat tighten. "I was afraid I'd missed it," she said.

"No, you didn't miss it."

"This is the bus to the Valley, I hope."

"I'm afraid so."

"Why do you say that?"

Phil shook his head. "I just don't like it. Too many curves. A bus on this route crashed, you know."

"Really?" Her frown returned, creasing the smooth skin between her eyebrows.

"Yes," Phil said. "It happened about a year ago. The bus ran off the road, up near Mulholland. It went over the side, down into one of the canyons."

"Oh, that's awful. Were people . . . hurt?"

"Everyone on the bus was killed."

She bared her teeth as if she were in pain. "I wish you hadn't told me that."

"I'm sorry. I didn't mean to upset you. By the way, my name is Phil."

"I'm Wendy."

"As in *Peter Pan*?"

She laughed softly. "Oh yes, I'm afraid

so. But I haven't sewn on any shadows lately, and I can't fly—not even with a sprinkling of pixie dust."

"That's a pity."

"Hey, if I could fly, I wouldn't be messing around with this stupid bus."

"You could just zoom on home."

Her mouth made a swooshing sound as she darted an open hand toward the sky. "Just like that. Don't I wish. Buses give me the creeps."

"Why is that?"

She shrugged her slender shoulders. "I don't know. Just 'cause they're full of strangers, I guess. And I mean some are *strange* strangers, not always your normal everyday people. I stay clear of buses, whenever I can. It's just that my car's in for repairs, or you wouldn't catch me dead on a bus. You never know when some oddball is going to sit down next to you and start talking crazy. To himself, more often than not."

"Would you mind sitting with me?" Phil asked.

"Promise not to talk to yourself?"

"Word of honor."

Grinning, she said, "Well then, you've got a deal." She leaned forward and glanced down the avenue. "Ah, here it comes. It wasn't so late."

It's later than you think, Phil thought.

T he doors of the bus folded open. Phil stepped ahead of Wendy. As he lifted a foot onto the step, the driver shook his head so hard his fat cheeks wobbled. "What's the matter with you, bud? Never heard of ladies first?"

"I don't mind," Wendy said.

"Yeah? Well, I do. Mind your manners, bud, or you can find yourself another bus."

"All right," Phil said. "Sorry." He stepped down and moved aside to let Wendy pass. He watched her climb the steps. There was a sudden gust of wind, and her skirt seemed to float up around her slim legs. She stopped beside the driver and dropped coins into the fare box.

The door started to shut.

Phil leaped into the gap. The rubber edge of the door slammed against him, but he forced his way through.

The driver smiled at him. "Sorry, bud, but you better get out."

"What for?"

Wendy, still standing near the fare box, looked down at Phil as if confused.

"The bus is full," the driver said.

Taking a step upward, Phil peered down the aisle. There were no more than ten or twelve passengers. Most of the seats were empty.

"What are you trying to pull?" Phil said angrily.

"You heard me," the driver said. "Off the bus, bud."

Phil stood his ground. "No way. If you want me off, you'll have to throw me off." He stepped up to the driver, his fists ready for action. "Do you want to give it a try?"

A corner of the driver's mouth curled up in a sneer. "Aah, go ahead and take a seat. No skin off my nose."

Phil put his fare into the box and followed Wendy down the aisle. "How about here?" he asked, nodding toward two empty seats beside the exit door.

"Here's fine," Wendy said.

They sat down facing the aisle. Wendy smoothed her skirt over her knees, and folded her hands. Phil took a deep breath, enjoying the smell of her perfume. Her shoulder pressed against him for a moment as the bus lurched forward.

"That driver's a weirdo," she said, scrunching up her face to look crazy.

"He's a complete lunatic."

"I thought you two were going to get into a brawl."

"I would've won."

"Why didn't he want you on the bus?"

"I guess he doesn't like my manners."

Smiling, she said in a gruff voice, "Never heard of ladies first?"

"Sorry about that. Like I said, though, he's a lunatic. He's tried to keep me off before. That's why I tried to get on ahead of you. One time he shut the door in my face and left without me."

"You ought to report him."

Phil shrugged. "It wouldn't do any good."

Suddenly the bus made a left turn so fast that the shopping bag of a man seated up the aisle slid off the seat. It hit the floor and fell over. An orange tumbled out and rolled away. Mumbling to himself, the man stood up to chase it.

The driver scowled over his shoulder. "Stay seated while the bus is moving!"

"But my orange!"

"You heard me, bud! If you don't like it, I'll put you off the bus."

The man's lips pressed together tightly, and he picked up his bag. Then he dropped back into his seat.

As the orange rolled down the aisle, Wendy stretched out a leg. The orange bumped against the side of her shoe. She reached down quickly and picked it up. The man who had lost it smiled at her. She tossed it to him. As he reached up and caught it with both hands, some of the passengers clapped. Wendy smiled beautifully and started to settle back in her seat.

The driver stomped on the brake pedal. The force of the bus stopping threw Phil sideways against Wendy. She gasped and slapped a hand against the seat cushion to stop her fall.

The driver leaped from his seat. Snarling, he shook a finger at Wendy. "I *saw* that! I'll have no food thrown on my bus!"

Outside, car horns were blaring.

"What's the matter with you!" he snapped at Wendy.

Wendy stared at him. Her face was red.

"Come on my bus and start throwing food!"

"You're a creep," she said.

Passengers clapped. The man with the orange clapped loudest of all. The driver's eyes were almost popping out of his head. "Shut up!" he yelled. "Everybody shut up!" Shaking his fists in the air, he started down the aisle toward Wendy.

Phil stood up. "Sit down and drive," he said.

"*You* again," the driver muttered. But he stopped walking. He stared at Phil, panting as if he were short of breath.

"Go on!" somebody called from behind them. "Sit down and drive."

"Yeah," called someone else.

"Crazy idiot," said another voice.

Everyone on the bus started yelling at the driver.

He shook a fist. "You'll get it! You'll all get it!" Then he whirled away and returned to his seat. The bus lurched forward.

Phil sat down. Wendy, smiling at him, patted his knee. "You were terrific," she said.

He looked into her eyes. They held his

gaze for a long time. "Terrific enough for a kiss?" he whispered.

Her smile slipped away. She nodded. Phil leaned close and gently kissed her mouth.

"Knock it off back there!" the driver yelled. "You think I don't see that?"

"Do you live in the Valley?" Wendy asked.

"Yes, in Studio City."

"I live in Sherman Oaks."

"Well, we're almost neighbors," Phil said, and squeezed her hand.

She stared into his eyes. "Maybe we could . . . get together sometime."

"I'd like that very much, Wendy."

She smiled. "Why don't I give you my phone number?" She took a ballpoint pen and a small pad from her purse. As she started to write, the bus stopped. She quickly finished putting down her name and telephone number, tore off the paper, and handed it to Phil.

Just then rock music filled the bus.

The driver yelled, "Turn off that blaster!"

Phil folded the paper neatly and slipped it into his shirt pocket. And in a loud voice, so he could be heard over the loud music, he said, "Thank you."

"Turn it off!" the driver shouted.

A teenage boy, paying no attention, strolled down the aisle. He carried the big radio on one shoulder, and snapped the fingers of his free hand in time with the beat.

Suddenly the bus shot forward. With a startled look on his face, the boy stumbled and fell down. His radio slammed against the floor. But it didn't break. Music kept on roaring from its twin speakers. He picked it up, and crawled to the nearest seat.

Wendy rolled her eyes upward as if to ask, "What next?"

The bus picked up speed. Turning to the window behind him, Phil saw the lighted fronts of shops race by. A moment later, the headlights of cars on a cross-street rushed at him. The bus got by just in time.

Over his shoulder, the driver cried, *"I'll teach you!"* His eyes were wide, his mouth twisted in a crazy grin. *"Oh yes, I'll teach you good!"* He hunched over the steering wheel.

The radio went silent. The sound of its music was replaced by the driver's mad laughter.

The boy, radio hugged to his chest, gazed at the man's back. "Hey," he called. "I turned it off. Slow down, would you? Please!"

The driver neither slowed the bus nor stopped his laughter.

The man with the grocery bag grabbed the nearest upright post and held it tightly.

Someone in the rear was tugging the bell cord. It rang and rang, a signal to stop the bus. But the bus didn't stop.

People shouted. A woman was crying.

The bus moved faster and faster. It tilted upward as the road climbed into the hills.

Wendy squeezed Phil's hand so hard it hurt. She looked at him. There was a look of terror in her eyes.

"Don't be afraid," Phil said.

"He's gonna get us killed!"

"We'll be all right," he said, but he didn't believe his own words.

"We've gotta *do* something!" she cried.

The boy across the aisle set his radio on the floor. He got to his feet and grabbed a handrail. His body swayed as the bus swung around a curve. Then he charged forward.

The driver yelled, "Stay seated while the bus is moving!" Then he cackled wildly and spun the steering wheel. The bus swerved, throwing the boy sideways. He fell against an empty seat, pushed himself up, and rushed the rest of the way up to the front.

The driver twisted around and drove an elbow into the boy's stomach. Doubling over, the boy stumbled backwards and fell in the aisle. His head crashed against one of the metal posts. He slumped to the floor and didn't move.

"I taught him!" the driver yelled in a gleeful voice, grinning over his shoulder. "Don't any of you try it again! I'll make us crash! That'll fix you!"

"What are we going to do?" Wendy asked.

Phil put an arm around Wendy and held her close to him. He could feel her shaking. "There's not much we *can* do," he told her. "You heard what the driver said. He'll make us crash if anyone tries to jump him."

"He'll crash, anyway, if he keeps going like this."

Phil said nothing. He held Wendy more tightly. He stared at their reflections in the window across the aisle. Wendy was leaning against him, her head down. He wished he could make her fear go away, but he didn't know how.

Beyond the windows was the dark hillside. Soon, he knew, it would fall away and there would be nothing on that side of the road except a steep drop-off to the ravine far below.

Wendy sat up straight. She turned her frightened eyes to Phil. "We have to try something," she said. She started to stand, but he pulled her down. "We have to . . ."

"He'll *do* it," Phil said. "He'll run us off the road."

"He'd be killing *himself*!"

"Don't you understand? He's crazy."

"But we can't just . . ." Her eyes opened wide. She leaned close to Phil and whispered, "We'll crawl. That way, he can't see us in his mirror. When we get close, I'll . . ." She frowned slightly. She grabbed her purse and pulled out her ballpoint pen. She clutched it like a knife. "I'll stab him with this. Right in the neck. You grab the steering wheel to keep us on the road, and try to turn off the engine."

"It won't work," Phil said.

"It might. Come on, we've got to *try*."

"All right," he said. He glanced forward. The driver had stopped laughing and was bent over the wheel, peering out the windshield.

Wendy slipped to the floor. Phil dropped down quickly. Side by side, they squirmed slowly up the aisle. The bus continued its mad race up the road, its tires squealing as it took the curves too fast. Phil looked at Wendy. Her lower lip was clamped between her teeth. Wisps of blond hair brushed against her forehead. Her eyes met his, and she smiled bravely. Phil turned his face away so that she wouldn't see the tears suddenly filling his eyes.

As they made their way forward, their shoulders touched. Phil wished he could take her into his arms and kiss her one more time.

When he looked at her again, he almost smiled. She had the plastic pen between her teeth like a pirate's knife.

They were only a yard behind the driver's seat.

Wendy took the pen from between her teeth, gripping it so tightly that her knuckles turned white, and nodded.

They both leaped up.

The driver gasped as they attacked. He jerked the wheel. The bus swerved, its headlights sweeping toward the low guard rail. Phil tugged the wheel toward him. The bus turned back into its lane. As he struggled to hold on, he saw Wendy hook an arm around the driver's head. She pulled it backward and stabbed at the man's neck. The pen struck his shoulder, and broke in half. Growling, he smashed an elbow into Phil's hip. The blow gave him a shock of pain, but he kept his grip. The bus swung wildly as the two men fought for control of the steering wheel.

Wendy, throwing away the pen, twisted the driver's head sideways and slammed a fist again and again into his face. Blood streamed from his nose. He squirmed and growled, but wouldn't let go of the wheel.

Phil glanced toward the back of the bus. If some of the other passengers would help . . . But the teenage boy was still out cold, and nobody else was coming forward. The rest were huddled in their seats. Some were crying. Others screamed as the bus swung from side to side.

The driver was too strong for Phil. The wheel was slipping through his fingers.

Letting go with one hand, he reached for the ignition key. An elbow rammed into his belly. His breath gushed out. As he gasped for air, the driver twisted toward him and shoved with both hands.

Phil was flung backwards. He tumbled down the stairs, his back hitting the door. As he struggled to get up, he saw the driver reach for the shiny handle that would open the door.

"No!" he cried out.

Wendy grabbed the driver's wrist, but his fingers wrapped around the handle and he pulled.

The door behind Phil folded open. He dropped away into the night. He landed in some bushes and began rolling downhill, as the bus shot past him. He bounced off a tree trunk, and yelled in pain.

Pushing himself to his feet, he watched the bus break through the guard rail. It seemed to hang in the air for a long time, its tail lights glowing red in the darkness like the eyes of a strange beast. Then it plunged out of sight.

There was no sound of a crash.

Phil limped across the road. He leaned against the guard rail and stared at the ravine below. There were no flames. There was no bus. He put his fingers into his shirt pocket, and felt for the paper with Wendy's name and telephone number. His pocket was empty. He knew it would be.

It was the first Friday night of the next month. Phil Archer sat down on the bench. The young woman at its other end glanced at him and then leaned forward and peered down the busy avenue. Phil looked, too. The bus was not yet in sight.

"It's never on time," he said.

Her fine eyebrows lifted in surprise. She smiled in a way that made Phil's throat tighten. "I was afraid I'd missed it," she said.

"No, you didn't miss it," Phil told her.

She was always here, the first Friday of the month. She never missed the bus. And, though the driver always tried to keep him off, Phil never missed it, either.

This would be his fourteenth ride. It would be much the same as the others. No matter what he tried, Wendy always boarded the bus. And moments later after he fell out, the bus always crashed.

Just as it had crashed the first time, more than a year ago.

He wished he had known Wendy before the awful accident took her life. That was impossible, of course.

But one night each month, for half an hour, he could sit with her and talk to her, hold her hand and kiss her. That was good enough. It had to be.

Wendy smiled at him. "This is the bus to the Valley, I hope."